HERE IN SANCTUARY—WHIRLING

Here in Sanctuary—
Whirling

D. Dina Friedman

Querencia Press, LLC
Chicago Illinois

QUERENCIA PRESS

© Copyright 2024
D. Dina Friedman

ISBN 978 1 959118 79 4

Cover Photo: D. Dina Friedman
.

www.querenciapress.com

First Published in 2024

Querencia Press, LLC
Chicago IL

Printed & Bound in the United States of America

ALSO BY D. DINA FRIEDMAN

Immigrants
Wolf in the Suitcase
Escaping Into the Night
Playing Dad's Song

For the children at the border camp in Matamoros, Mexico
and the children at the detention center in Homestead, Florida

and all children everywhere with big dreams

CONTENTS

MIRA

Mira, he cries. *Look!*
Puddles have grown into rivers.

The *rio* cannot be held
in its banks. *Mira!*

We are brothers in the flood.
Hermanos. Familias.

Families here, *Señor*
el Presidente. Mira. Look. *Niños*.

Have you seen *los hombres del gobierno?*
Pontificating balloons.

Do you have a pin?
Let the floodgates open!

Hope is a river wearing down rocks,
a child's pair of striped overalls hanging on barbed wire,

a voice rising from the water crying, *Mira.*
Míranos!

HERE IN SANCTUARY—WHIRLING

I.

The room in the stone church is always cold, always with disengaged puzzle pieces on the table. It's the only time I do puzzles, though it's hard to see the nuances of color in the basement light. This is where Lucio, whose name means light, has been harbored for two years, a place where the sun ruptures into bits of nothing as it tries to break through the windows.

II.

On the computer, I discover a painting of a twirling girl in a patterned hijab of bright, bold colors. The veil covers the entire top of her body like a cape. Underneath she wears patterned leggings whose background is the color of night. The two halves of her body grate against my eye's need for harmony, so I keep my focus on the tresses of the hijab, which fold over themselves in mid-twirl.

III.

I have learned that the shape matters more than the color in doing puzzles. Especially when there are countless pieces of burnt orange. Or a section that's nothing but black.

IV.

The girl in the painting reminds me of the whirling dervishes in Turkey. When they spun, it looked as if their eyes had receded to some distant point in the murky center of their brains. They always wore white, and they whirled in a bar that sold forbidden wine. Lucio waves at me as he whirls through the hall on his way to help with the soup kitchen. Spatula in hand, he reminds me of that famous painting, American Gothic.

V.

A long time ago, at a Sufi dancing class, I whirled and chanted the name of Allah. It felt like I was talking to the same God I knew, but dressed in a different costume. If the girl in the picture takes off the hijab, are there more patterns underneath, or essence?

VI.

If I ask Lucio how he is, he will always tell me he is fine, *graciás a Diós*.

VII.

A longer time ago, I whirled in my grandmother's living room, which also had dark walls and no light. I can't remember if I got dizzier when I closed my eyes or when I kept them open. I do remember spinning to the point of tipsiness, though I never fell.

VIII.

Here, at the sanctuary, I always feel like I'm falling as I tackle the puzzle, maneuvering bump into hole, bump into hole. Why are the puzzle pieces so pastoral, flowers or barns with nothing out of kilter, pleasing to the cliché-driven eye?

IX.

At the point where the hijab ends and the leggings begin, the girl's palms are open, as if she's expecting the air of God to fall into her hands.

NOTE FROM THE AIRBNB IN TEXAS: *PLEASE DON'T KILL THE SPIDER*

He has a name: Septimus,
because he lost a leg somewhere.

You might find him by the toilet.
Don't shriek as you do your doo.

His poison is all in your head.
Didn't you read *Charlotte's Web?*

Humble is the word that matters.
Confront your failings. Take a selfie,

if you're lucky enough to spot him.
And put on your boots, hat.

This is cowboy country,
land of brash bravado.

Where's your gun?
A spider could be lurking under your pillow.

Unseen children taken at the border:
their parents' lost limbs.

I'VE JUST FOLDED THIS POEM INTO AN AIRPLANE

I.

To prepare for flight, I deepen the crease, rip off a piece of the corner, spit on the wing for luck. I fling the paper toward the fence, which is covered with black sheathing. There's a sign on the black that says "no trespassing."

On the other side of the fence, boys wear orange hats.

II.

Will my plane make it over the border? Will one of the boys catch my plane in his orange hat?

Or will the man with the biceps who stands by his police car making videos intercept my plane and kick it into the gutter? He is making videos because we are standing on ladders, holding up hearts on long sticks so the boys can see them.

III.

Should I send this poem to airplane makers, since this used to be an Air Force base before it became a prison for children in orange hats?

We used to think school was a prison because the desks were bolted to the floor. We weren't allowed to sail paper airplanes in school, but sometimes the boys got wild and threw them anyway. They got sent to the principal's office.

IV.

Sometimes the boys wave their orange hats at us and curl their hands into the shape of a heart.

Sometimes we hug and kiss in front of the bicep man to make the videos more interesting. We can't hug the children. The children can't hug each other.

V.

We don't see the girls. We heard they only come out when there's no one on the ladders to hold up hearts or write poems and fold them into paper airplanes. It's always that way when it comes to treating girls.

I would like to talk to the girls. I would like to talk to the bicep man making the videos. I say good morning to him, but he doesn't answer. I say good afternoon to him. He doesn't answer.

VI.

In school, our children have written letters to the children in the orange hats. We bring the children's letters to the bicep man. The bicep man says he can't take the letters. Everything needs to be checked for poison powder.

This is why we have to fold the letters into paper airplanes and sail them over the fence. How to fold a thousand letters into paper airplanes, like a thousand paper cranes?

VII.

Before the launch, we make videos of the letters in case they don't arrive. They are filled with pictures of houses and dogs and funny robots.

One letter says, "Hola amigo. I was an immigrant like you, but now I'm here. I'm happy."

REFUGEE CAMP: MATAMOROS

A small boy braving the rain
sways on the banks of the *Rio Bravo*.

What does he remember of his home in Honduras
before the men broke windows,

took his sister's doll,
his father's heart.

Now, a doll with a dismembered arm
hangs naked on the barbed wire fence.

Behind the grates, people cook *tortillas, platanos,*
arroz con pollo on small stoves.

We balance our bodies on broken chairs.
With broken Spanish, we piece the words

of the woman who fled
because they said they'd kill her son,

that boy too close
to the edge of the river.

There's a church here
with books about Jesus,

who's white in all the pictures,
like the ladies serving on the dinner line.

Only the children are smiling.
Everyone wants more water.

RUPTURES

It's raining.
My gums are bleeding.

The cover crop is in, trying to replenish
the barely fertile ground.

There's a line of hungry people
traveling north on the spine of America,

whose skin will be ripped by the river's barbed wire
if they try to swim across our border.

When will the next scab form
on the raw space between the teeth,

then detach
spurting more blood on the tongue?

On the day of her abrupted placenta,
my daughter asked me to go to her home,

clean blood off the floors. Hours later
the baby came, sweet-faced, sleepy.

Now he's pointing his finger
to ask for bananas, or to turn on the light.

MY FRIEND TELLS ME THERE ARE THOUSANDS OF STORIES JUST LIKE THIS ONE

Man who takes us to the Matamoros *mercado*
to buy food for *refugiados* to cook by their tents
tosses frosted flakes in the cart with the rice,
tells us he'll pay, man whose money
we wave away. It's a gift, *un regalo*.
Man whose glow is a *regalo*, scrolling
through phone to show us *mamá y papá*.
He left without time to say goodbye;
his *abuelita,* who now has died.
Man who says, you must understand,

I love my country, *amo mi país.*
I had a good job, never wanted to leave.
El año pasado, last year, on Valentine's Day
I called *mi esposa,* said, *Amor,* let's go out.
We took the kids and came back late,
fell happy, full of love, into our beds.
In the middle of dreams, a noise in the night,
man with a mask, black hat with holes for eyes.
When I tussled with the guy, the mask
came off; I saw a boy I knew,
then the others surging with the guns.
I told them to take whatever they wanted.
The next day, I went to *la policía.* All they wanted
was my phone number. I'd barely gone a kilometer
when the phone rang with *amenazas de muerte,* threats of death.

Man on planks of wood, lashed
to an inner tube, crosses the river to Mexico
in the dead of night when the guards are gone,
each daughter held in a muscled arm.
Man riding on bus after bus, north
to *la frontera*, bad *hombres* lurking in the shadows.
The guards block the way, the only *opción*
to pay the *coyote* to take his wife
and younger daughter. (He didn't have enough
for all to go together.) On the opposite
shore, man's wife presents herself to ICE.
She's put in the "*hielera*," where the detainees shiver,
then sent to the midwest to live with her brother.
She is one of the lucky ones.

Man raises money to cross with *coyote,*
asks for asylum and is taken with daughter,
put in the *hielera*, three days. Couldn't bathe.
They blast sirens in the night to prevent you from sleeping.
His beary arms couldn't stop his daughter's shivering.
He thought they'd send him to his *familia,*
but they took him to Tijuana, so he could wait in Mexico.
Man who refused to go. Said,
I won't sign these *papeles*. They marked him
troublemaker and sent him there anyway.
Man whose daughter *tenía hambre*, so hungry.
When he tells us this part, he starts to cry.

Man whose arm I touch, chasms away in his *dolor privado,*
los memorias that could shackle a thousand hearts.

Man who clung to his daughter when the gangs grabbed her
and shoved them both in a car, demanding ransom,
which his wife had to borrow to pay. They dumped him
far away in the desert, across the border,
where for hours they wandered in the dark, coyotes howling,
until they found a woman, an angel he thought,
who fed them and led them to the city, where she stuck
out her palm for money, and they were forced into another car.
He should have known the world, like the wall
at the border, is lined with spikes. Man held

for money, then more money, until all sucked dry.
If his wife didn't pay, they said they'd kill him.
In a last gasp he retrieves the hidden,
maybe broken, phone in his daughter's teddy bear,
with only a battery sliver, texts the location
to *su esposa,* who calls the cops,
who come and find seven more people
captured there, all put back
in the *hielera,* all sent back to Mexico,
where they all wait, all hope. *Esperar.*
In Spanish, it's the same word.

STATUE OF LIBERTY

I.

You can't really forget a green statue, because when you're a kid you know that statues aren't supposed to be Comet-vomit-green. We took a boat. I was little, maybe four or five, and I couldn't see over other people's heads. We might have gone into the statue, but maybe we didn't because the line was too long and my mother hates waiting in lines. My mother told me you used to be able to go all the way to the torch, but they closed that part off because someone fell, or maybe they jumped. I looked up at the torch and felt cheated. That's the only part I remember.

II.

I took my boyfriend here when I was in college. He was from suburban Illinois, a land of people who were tall, white, and blond. It was a windy day in January, so the boat was nearly empty. We couldn't go into the statue because it was closed for renovations. Or maybe we went in and walked up all those stairs to look out the crown's windows to the harbor, and beyond to the open sea. To tell the truth, I don't remember. To tell the truth, I couldn't see over my boyfriend's head.

III.

I broke up with my boyfriend because he was blond. That's the simplified version of the story, though perhaps I broke up with him because he was from not-New York, or because the Statue of Liberty was closed the day I took him there. I broke

25

up with my best friend several years earlier, when I was still in high school. She was the Chinese daughter of immigrants. We were on the subway. She was reading Ayn Rand. I told her I was a socialist and she stopped talking to me. Her stop came first. She got off the train and I watched the closing doors.

IV.

I never thought I could leave New York, but I did. Breaking up with New York was harder than leaving my blond boyfriend and harder than the day my best friend stopped talking to me. Now I'm living on a farm with tall, blond people and a lot of cows. The cows have the illusion of freedom in the pasture until they graze by the electric fence.

V.

During these difficult days there have been many cartoons of the Statue of Liberty being violated. There's one with the immigrant-hating president ripping off her head and holding it as a trophy. There's another where she has a For Sale sign hung around her neck. I visit New York, but I don't go to the statue. Instead, I go to protest the immigrant-hating president in front of his big skyscraper. Before he was elected, they put a statue of him naked with diaper rash and a sagging potbelly in Union Square. The statue wasn't green, but maybe it should have been.

VI.

Once I went with my children to the Statue of Liberty, but they were bored and we didn't go inside. Or maybe we did go inside and they were bored. Or maybe we just went to Ellis Island, where I remember with certainty that they were bored, even when we found the plaques my parents paid for, which had the names of our great-great-grandparents, who came to the Statue of Liberty on crowded boats where they couldn't see over people's heads. It's hard sometimes to raise children in a land of blond people with too many cows.

VII.

My great-great-grandmother came here to escape the pogroms. My great grandmother told me her mother said that whenever the Cossacks came to the door, she would make the sign of the cross and say, "Christians Live Here," or maybe my grandmother told me that story about her grandmother. I don't remember. What I do remember is they both said the Old Country was very bad. Other people I went to school with were children of Holocaust survivors. We played a game in the schoolyard called Concentration Camp. It was kind of like tag, except the "it" person was the Nazi, and if they caught you, they made you do unspeakable second-grade things. In school we sang, "My Country 'Tis of Thee," and "God Bless America." One year we did an assembly program called "Sing, America, Sing." I wrote a satire called, "Cry, America, Cry." Even then, I was a socialist.

VIII.

I have just returned from the refugee camp in Matamoros, Mexico, where there is no Statue of Liberty. Instead, there's a tall guard at the bridge who won't let anyone put a foot in the country to claim asylum or see over his head. A man in the camp tells me of intruders coming to his house with guns. He tells me about being shoved into a car with his eight-year-old daughter by kidnappers demanding ransom. He tells me about being taken by immigration authorities and locked in a cold, windowless room. At least, the statue still has windows. I did climb it at least once. I remember clearly the day I looked out through the dirty glass.

VALENTINE

A heart made of paper
will wrinkle
if you flail it

in the wind
on a ladder
watching children

playing soccer
on the other side
of a barbed wire fence.

When you wave your heart,
they'll lift their orange hats
like torches. And the guards

will tell them
you're being paid
to hold those silly hearts,

like those folks by Liberty Taxes,
costumed in the statue's crown,
who flap their arms,

waving you in
to pay
for caging

these children.
It's Valentine's Day,
or it will be

when the sun rises.
You're holding a heart
at an airport in Texas,

where you wait
for the cuffed children
to limp into the plane,

which crouches round-nosed:
a dolphin with the belly of a shark.
When the transport bus lights

appear out of fog,
you brandish your paper heart,
shout, *I love you.*

Once upon a time, Valentine's Day
was about pasting hearts on doilies
and eating chocolate.

You have a chocolate
to press into someone's hands;
when the bus stops,

you press yourself against its grille.
By the tinted window,
a shadow holds up shackled wrists,

fingers curved
into the unmistakable shape
of a heart.

BETHLEHEM

—After *In Tall Grass*, by Carl Sandburg

In the dead horse's head, the bees are making honey.
The grass is long and harbors ticks.
In Bethlehem, women stashed their babies

in caves, away from crazy King Herod,
who tried to kill their children, for fear
they might be gods. There's been a recent reveal

that ticks were engineered to carry Lyme,
an experiment in chemical weaponry. Soldiers searched
for the Bethlehem babies, carrying swords.

Did they kill by slicing the gut, the heart?
Did they cut the head, leaving it to the bees?
Did bees make honey in the babies' heads?

Were there flowers in the desert?
What was forgotten? The honeycomb,
the short lives of drones, and babies

who might have been gods? The wails
of mothers whose babies were seized?
The crazy king's queen,

killed out of jealousy? The queen bee,
dying when she finished making honey
in the horse's head? What's left?

The venomous bite of the tick.
The granddaughter, Salome,
her voracious appetite for heads on platters,

and the mad buzz of modern despots
who cage children crossing borders.
The dark jar of honey, the ticks, Uzis,

schoolyard children beheaded by bullets.
Are there flowers in the desert?
What will the wise men bring?

IT WAS THE MOST REMARKABLE DAY

We talked about wildfires, heaven and hell,
the late frost. Later, I roasted the remains
of the tomatillos, watched the latest revelation
on TV news: the wall at the border
sliceable with a hundred-dollar saw.
I doused parsnips like an arsonist,
rifled through pillars of carrots, onions
sealed in the basement container. The children

at the border are hungry. I imagine a carrot wall
like the witch house in Hansel and Gretel,
something with gnawable edges. Hell,
I should pack up these carrots
and take them to the border, like last summer,
on the ladder, waving at the children.
How to escort them out of hell? If I tell
their stories will they spread like wildfire,
burning our comfortable houses in their wake?
What are their mothers cooking over an open fire?

I will combine the parsnips with polenta,
add the roasted tomatillos and a touch of vinegar.
My salad, like the day, will be remarkable,
not for its taste, but for its failure
to cross a border, to be wildfire.

ON THE WHITEWATER: BIG BEND, TEXAS

The guide said we'll eat lunch in Mexico,
edged our raft to the eroding bank. No
sombreros. No place to buy burritos.
Spiny cactus on either side
of the Rio Grande / *Rio Bravo.*

The red-nailed woman in the cowboy-hat
unwrapped her pulled pork, and we glommed hummus
with lettuce, tomatoes. She asked us,
why do y'all call a White Elephant a Yankee Swap
then reminded herself we didn't mind being Yankees.

I reminded myself, people died
when they tried to cross to the *Yanqui* side
of the treacherous desert,

and scientists dressed dead pigs
to determine how fast the vultures
devoured the rotting bodies,
eating clothing, skin,
all the way to the viscera,
how skulls rolled alone
in the thorny flora
landing far from the crossers'
unidentified femurs.

Places are unfamiliar
if you let them be strangers.
Did they hear the Divine,
feel a hand on the shoulders

saying, *Keep walking,*
steady. Está bien.
It's all okay.

CUMBIA ON YOUTUBE

The beat burrows like a happy parasite.
A white woman dances with subtle shrugs.

In the next cut, the accordion player
drives through a desolate place, like our border,

where a man named Scott left jugs of water
for women and children, who crawled through the desert

like ants, but without a colony, and thirstier.
The police arrested him for aiding aliens.

When I was a kid, an alien was My Favorite Martian
or Mr. Spock. My child's partner tells of his mother,

a Republican lady in Iowa. When he pierced
his ears, she wailed, "How could you do this to me?"

Cumbia's accordion drives a mean polka.
Its throbbing beat evokes echoes of Africa,

lands overtaken—a familiar story. A toddler in Iowa
liked to sing while he peed down his slide.

The neighbor chided from the other side
of her gated yard. But the kid just crooned, *Go fuck yourself.*

Did he embarrass his mother? And what about Scott?
20-year sentence for a felony crime.

How could he do this to her?
How could he not?

THE PARTING

In this dream, my grandma is sulking
at the side of the sanctuary
where I've just given a speech
about immigrants at the border,
the river that separates them
from us, and how, like Moses,
we need to lift our rod
to move that water. My grandmother
is wearing polyester slacks
and a tunic, frosted blue. Her dark,
dyed hair clings to her scalp
as she shakes her head, no, at me,
like I'm four, reaching my hand
where it shouldn't be.

You're such a wimberduck,
she says, as I step off the *bimah*
to look for my shoes in a pile.
My grandmother has kept on her high
heels, but my shoes seem to be gone.
I kneel, sifting through army boots,
my short grandma towering over me,
uttering more nonsense words
about what I am, while I think about

all I'm not——the woman taking a knee
in front of those cops holding clubs.
I'm nothing but a stream of precious words
evaporated into air, yet the shame lingers
because I have displeased my grandmother.
If only I could feel a burning bush
in the exhale of people kneeling for their lives.
I might run in and save someone
before the clubs rain down. I might find,
inside myself, a rod to lift, waters to part.
But I'm stuck not seeing,
looking only for my shoes.

BECAUSE THE WIND IS RISING AND LAST WEEK THERE WAS A MICROBURST

Live in the layers / Not on the litter—Stanley Kunitz

I.

Carcasses of trees, severed from roots, fog the forward path.
We step over branches with browning leaves, chilled in the
poison breath of the wind.

II.

Soon the trunks will be shredded for lumber to keep the
machinery of the world running. My friend, so desperate, he
might send his daughter over the bridge alone to face the
guards at the border.

III.

How do we hold ourselves up when we're paper puppets in
the wind? Where my friend waits to cross, the river is rising
and the litter swirls. On my beautiful side of the planet, the
trees and wires are down. I am helpless to help him.

IV.

I picture my friend and his daughter in my home between the
mountain and the river, eating hot tomato soup and looking
out the window to gawk at the tree whose limb plunged in the
microburst, barely missing the roof.

V.

The forked branch landed by the front door, its crown of red leaves blocking the path. We thought we had an antidote for locked borders. We thought underneath the trunk of a uniform, a pathway to a softer heart.

VI.

The children whirl through the muddy camp like litter between layers of heartless words that leave no space for a sun drawn with a green marker on a scrap of paper grabbed from the gale.

VII.

Who am I to hug a dying tree? To smile because the sky is blue and the sun is shining? It's shredding day. I'll make tomato soup and freeze it for sparser times, then march the papers to the truck that splits them into litter, spaghetti in the wind.

POGROM

—for my great-great grandmother, Matilda

In the picture, your neck is rigid.
You have my grandmother's eyes,

her jaw, set on indestructible.
We are, after all, cut

from the same dark threads.
How did you feel when the knock

rattled your door? The man flaunting
his knife, smell of vodka in his sweat.

Did your breath catch
as he shoved in

and you made the sign of the cross
said, *Christians live here.*

He didn't care.
Flesh is flesh.

This may not have happened.
The story you told your daughter

uncovered only the barest
of the old country's bones.

43

What carried through our link
was simply the act of lying.

Your daughter grew up American, strange.
Her daughter had a Christmas tree.

Her daughter's daughter knew the bodies
that press against little girls on subways,

how to set her lips,
stifle the silent scream.

Now, I hold hearts to windows
where shackled women wait

to be shoved out of this land,
women with stories of daughters,

and men breaking into houses
holding knives to throats.

BECAUSE THE DEACON COULDN'T SLEEP

they disturbed the witch, grasped her wrists, dragged her,
armpits screaming, and strung her up
on a maple tree, tapped for syrup
in cooler months——a smudge of history

set before white hoods and burning
crosses. The insomniac
deacon, a supplicant. The woman,
a poor brute, dependent on alms,
who spoke, people said, with the devil's
tongue, her cat-shaped familiar
a specter discovered in the deacon's bed.
People said her spells bewitched the cows,
and when a chicken fell
into a neighbor's boiling pot,
she was the one who scalded.

II.
In the Florida sun, men curve
cat-backed as they scrape
damaged shards off a deacon's roof,
praying to Jesus for a better life.
These men, disturbed,
follow weather disasters, kneel
for a chance to fix what's ruined.
They secure the shingles, singing
a devil's rhythm, the neighbors say.

If a roof is wrecked, no one cares
about their papers, but when they ask
for pay, the deacon warns he'll call *la migra,*
closes his double door
to sleep in a cool white haze.

III.

Because we can sleep. Because
our roofs are shingled tight.
Because we think ourselves
too learned to believe

in demons, whether or not
we believe in God. We close doors,
hang "Do Not Disturb"
on flimsy plastic cards. Large letters.
Black against white.

I DO NOT KNOW

Why the wind is so fierce today. Why some people die
and others recover. Does a tornado choose its targets?
Is there a blueprint somewhere with the secret path
of my life mapped out? Will this trail I'm on
connect with the ridgeline, or will it keep crossing
the same stream? How do I get to the bunker,
and what's hidden there now that the army no longer has it?
I do not know how dirt feels to a carrot root, or to my brother
six feet under. Is he able to read the prayer books
placed on his coffin, through some double miracle
of semi-resurrection and dyslexia cured? What does it feel like
to a dyslexic when letters leave their prescribed places?
Why do bodies compartmentalize into people who love each other
hating the people across the river, who love each other
and hate the people across the river? Why do we have to teach
toddlers to share their sand-buckets? Why don't they do it naturally?
Why don't we do it naturally? Why don't we do it?

DETERMINATION

A yogi once told me,
raising legs above head

is about
convincing

the mind.

For now,
keep reaching.

In Matamoros today
the refugees are dancing,

parading effigies
of the defeated *presidente,*

eyes tracking
the wall where the flag flies,

hope, a focal point,
the *drishti.*

One leg stretched
toward a possible sky,

the other lifting
proudly.

HOPE

I feel you in my chest, soft as the young cat
stretched luxurious across the bed. Hope
in the dream of the next step, *esperanza:* a puff
of milkweed riding the wave of the wind.
Hope—*ku'lbal k'ux*—in the eyes of the woman
at the border-camp, the arch of her chin
lifting over the river where there once was a bridge.
Hope—*espwa*—keeps her facing forward,
even as she turns to me in the makeshift tent
called school, and spills her truth:
I can't write. I can't read.

What does it mean to simply listen,
transcribe her bursting words
as her dark-eyed baby smiles, then hides
bashful against his mother's breast? How
to reach across the river, jump like the cat
now sniffing at the open doorway,
one six-fingered paw pressing against the sill.

ACKNOWLEDGMENTS

Gratitude to the journals in which the following poems have appeared:

"Here in Sanctuary—Whirling," and "On the Whitewater: Big Bend, Texas," in *Naugatuck River Review*

"I've Just Folded this Poem Into an Airplane," "Refugee Camp: Matamoros," and "Valentine," in *Wordpeace*

"Statue of Liberty," in *Prose Online*

"Bethlehem," in *Twyckenham Notes*

"It was the Most Remarkable Day," in *Syracuse Cultural Workers 2022 Datebook*

"Because the Wind is Rising and Last Week There was a Microburst," in *The Bluebird Word*

"Because the Deacon Couldn't Sleep," in *Parcham*

"I Do Not Know," in *Silkworm*

Thank you to:

◊ *Emily at Querencia Press for sharing the vision and making this process a truly writer-centered experience.*

◊ *My awesome poetry group, whose kind, caring, perceptive and insightful feedback keeps me authentic and honest: Kol, Sarah, Lindsay, and Amy. And to the many people in my network of writing communities who have inspired me with your encouragement and your own important words.*

◊ *My compañeras in the Jewish Activists for Immigration Justice who traveled with me to the immigrant child detention center and the border camp: Susie, Betty, Carolyn, Joyce, Karen, Alice, Holly, David, Joan, Shel, and Annique.*

◊ *The immigration advocacy groups I encountered on this path whose compassion and perseverance continue to be inspirational: Witness at the Border, Team Brownsville, Angry Tias and Abuelas, Resource Center of Matamoros, Solidarity Engineering, Families Belong Together, Lawyers for Good Government—and, closer to home, those who worked tireless hours to provide sanctuary for endangered members of our community in western Massachusetts.*

◊ *And, most importantly, the people who trusted me with their stories and continue to touch my heart. For their safety, they will remain unnamed.*

Printed in the USA
CPSIA information can be obtained
at www.ICGtesting.com
LVHW041706280224
773024LV00062B/2003